# Th



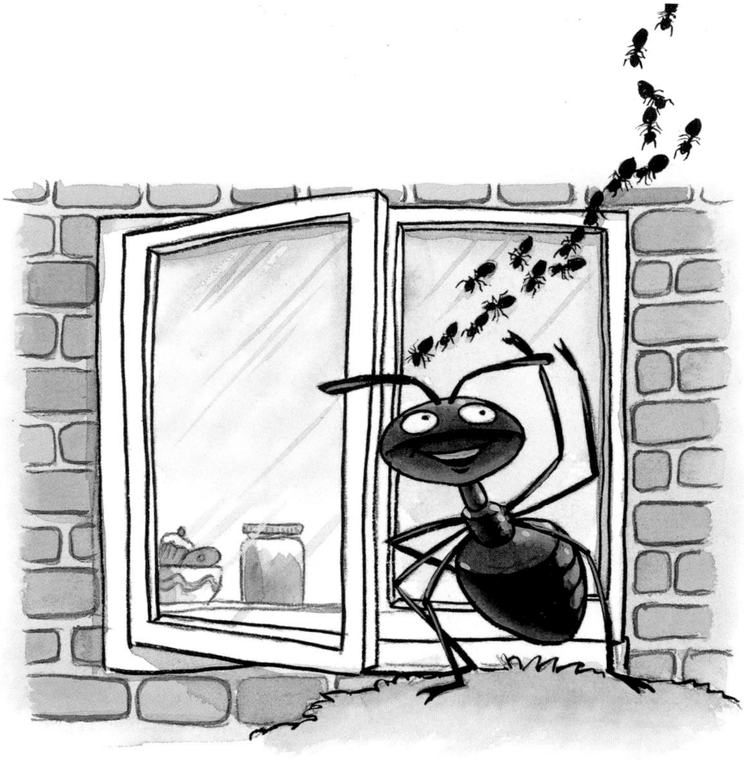

Illustrated by Dave Gunson

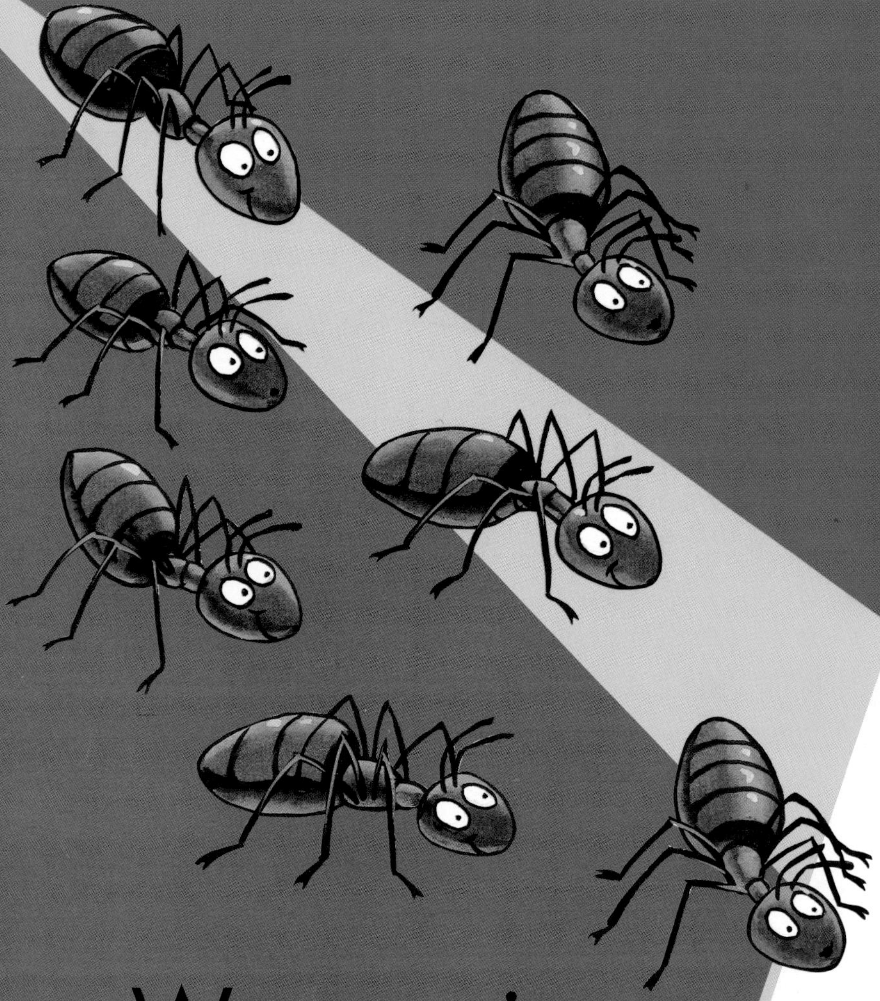

We go in
the jam.

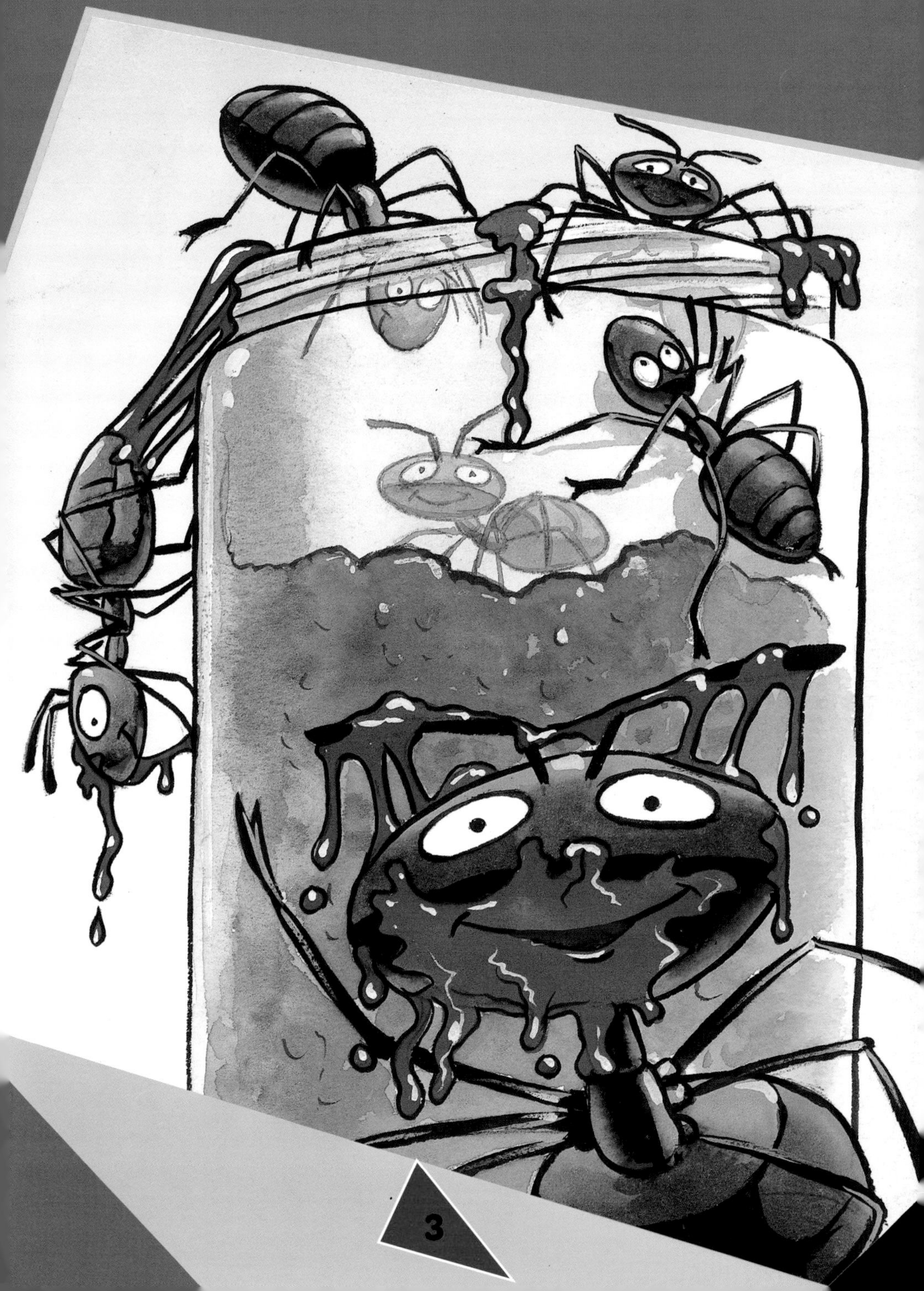

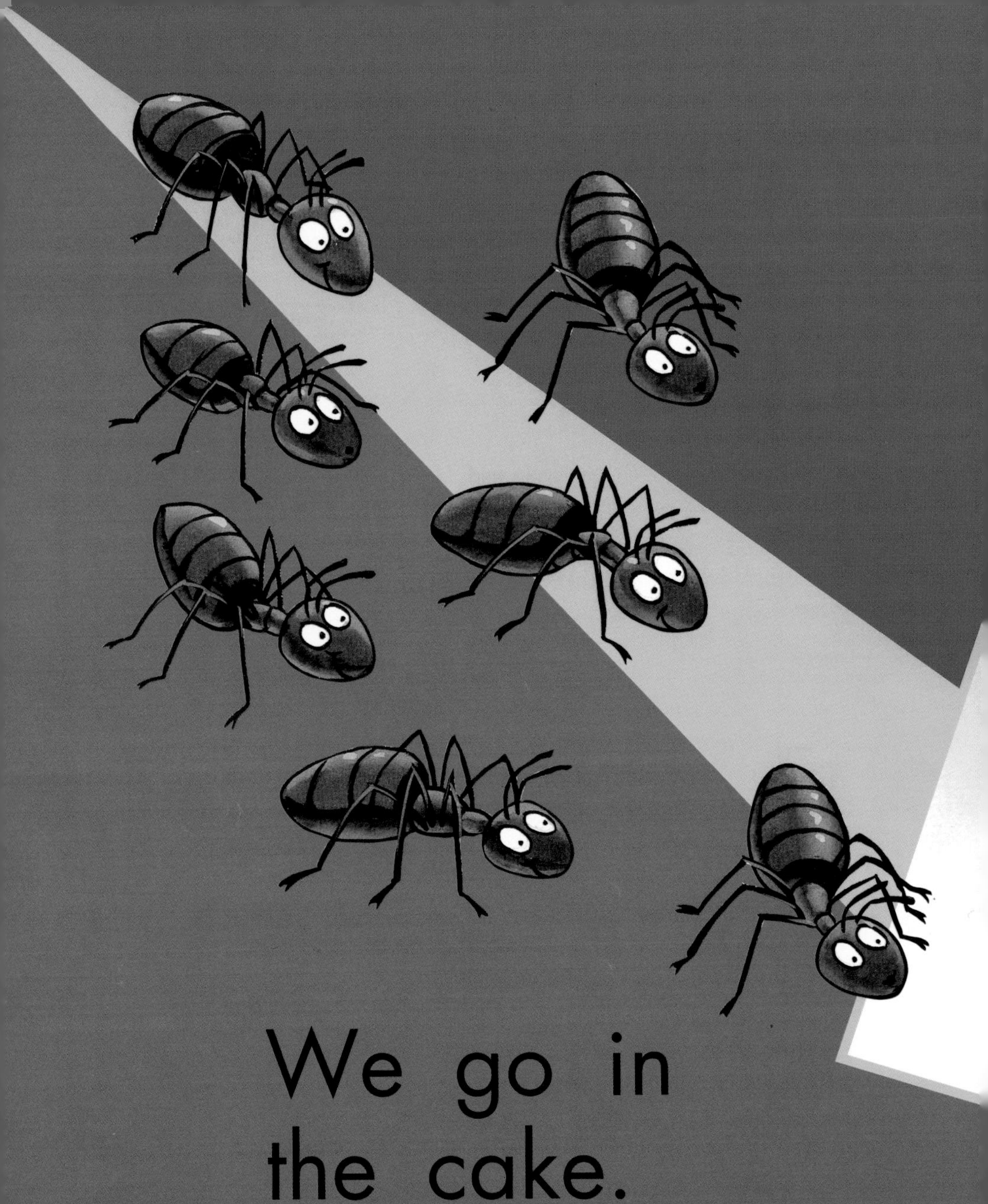

We go in the cake.

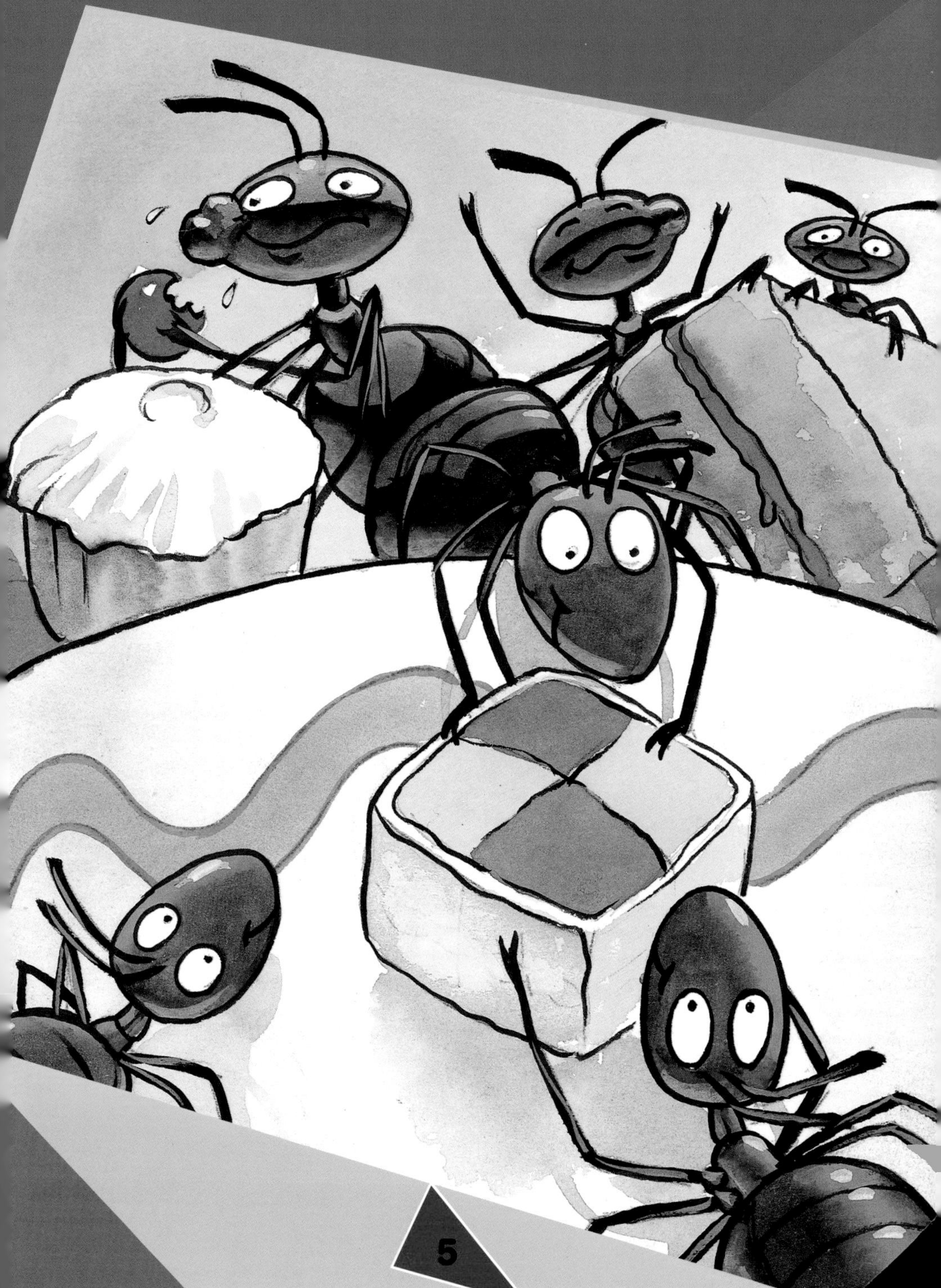

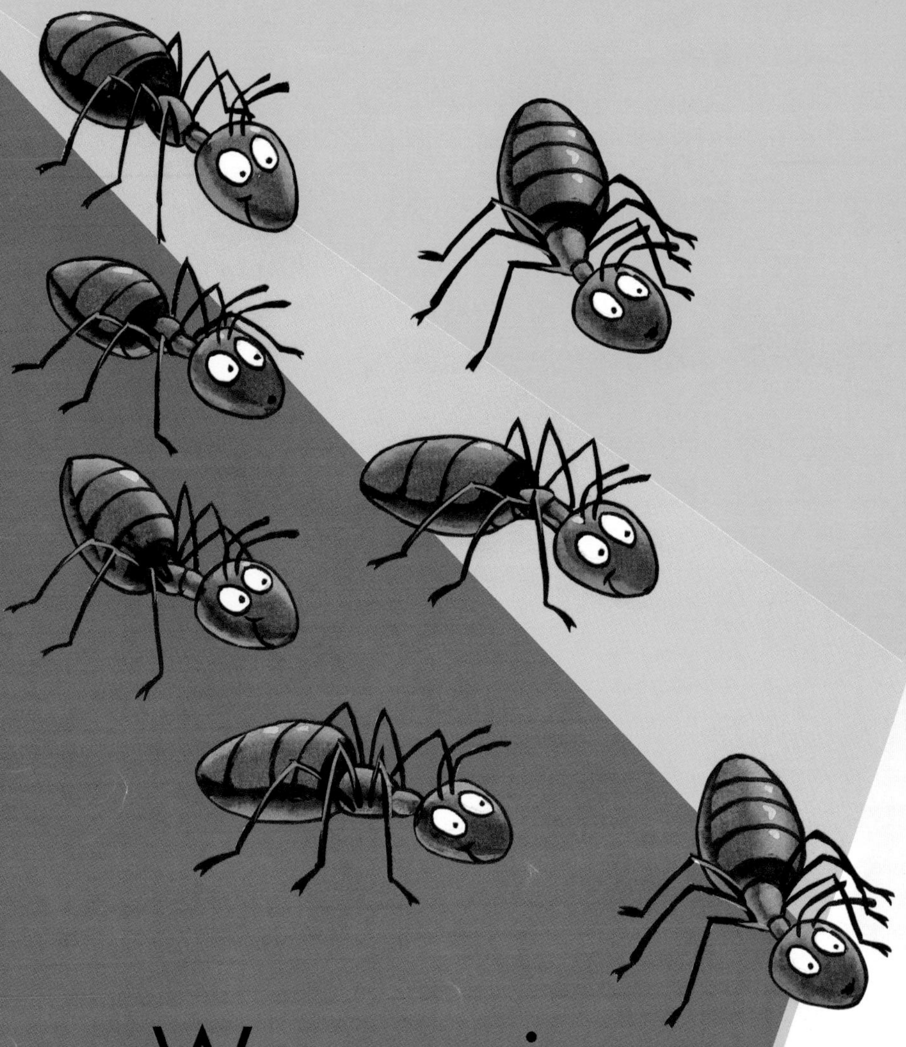

We go in
the cookies.

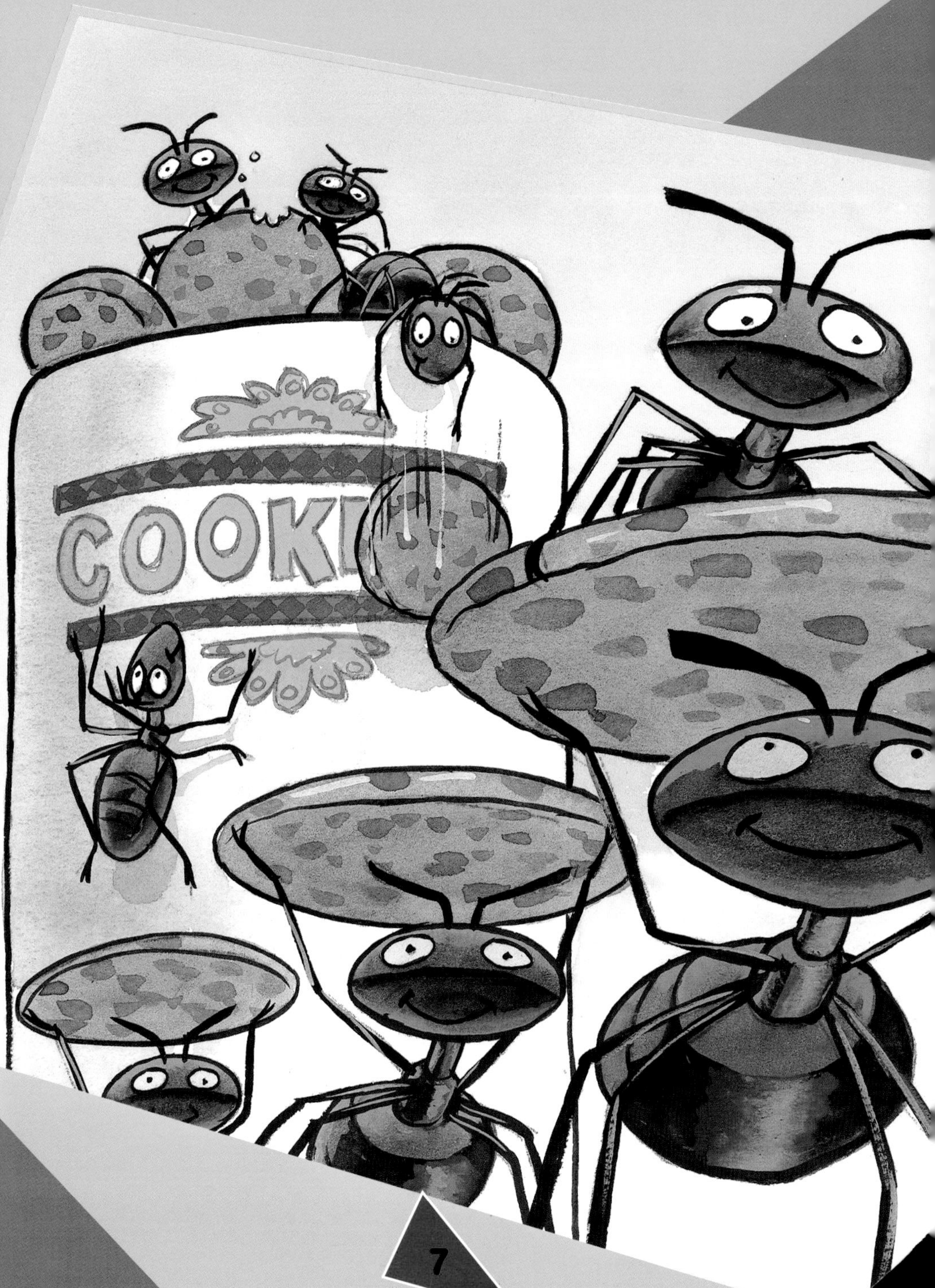
COOKI

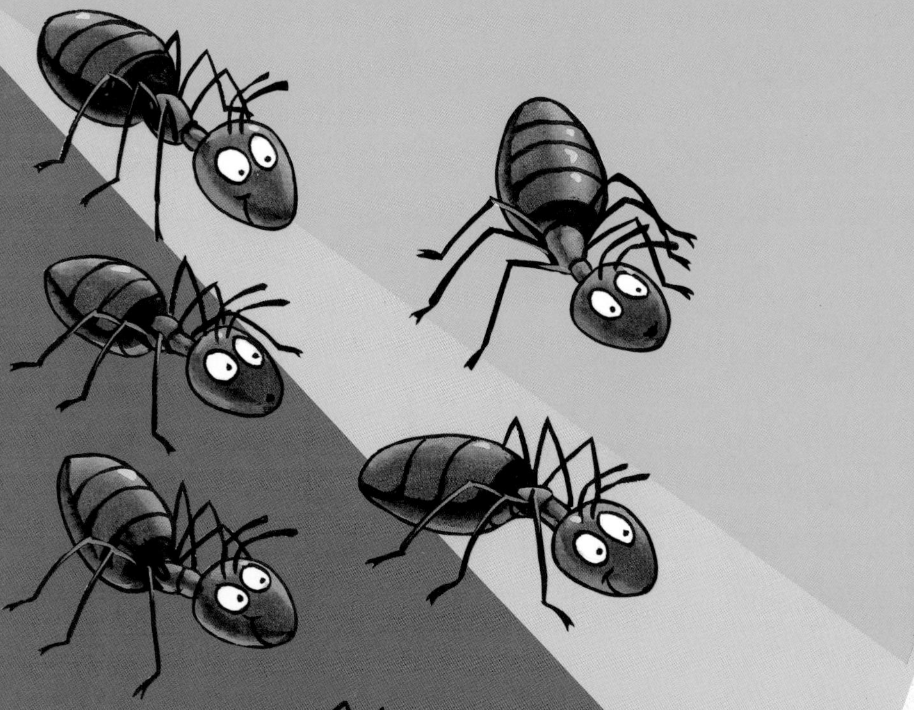

We go in
the apples.

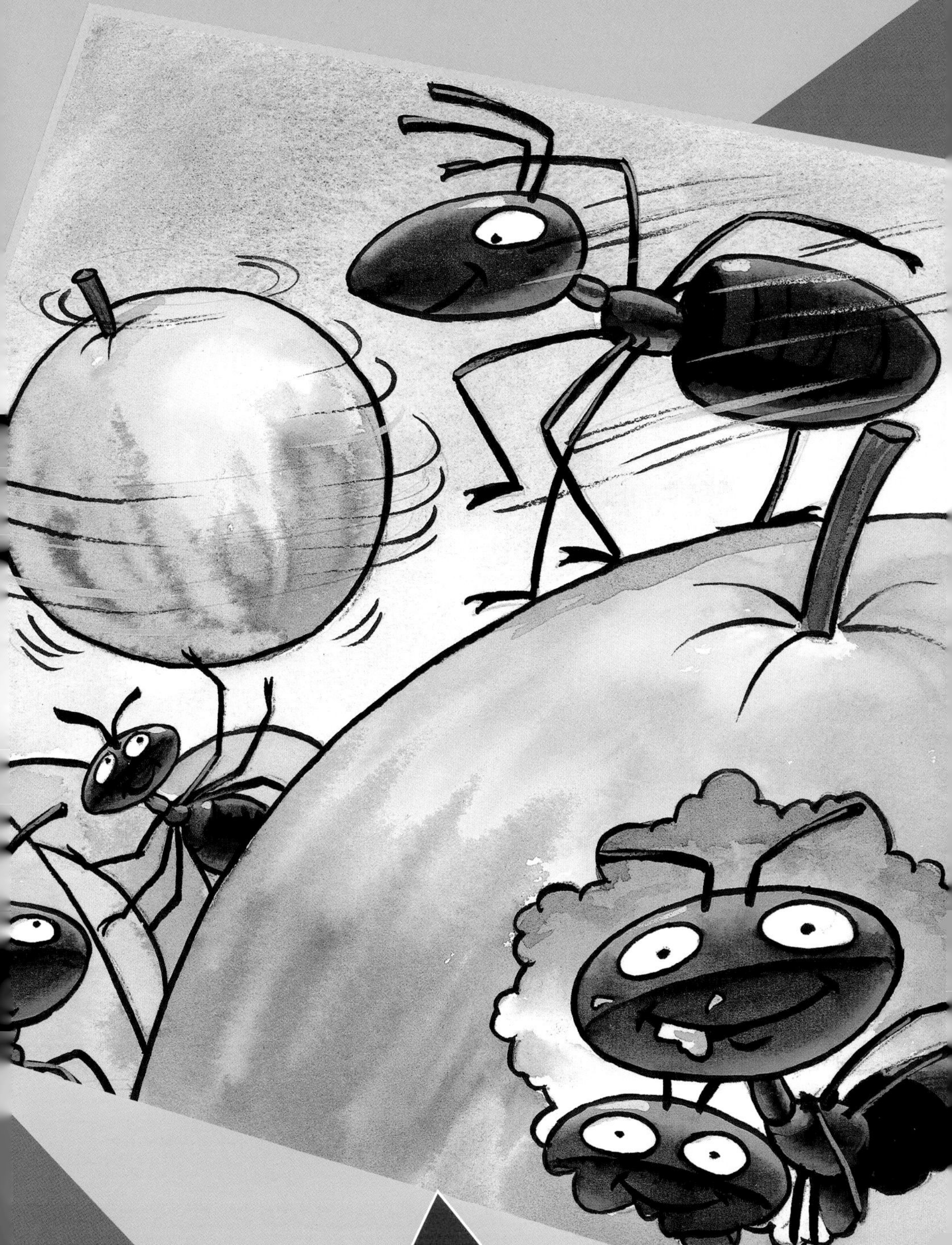

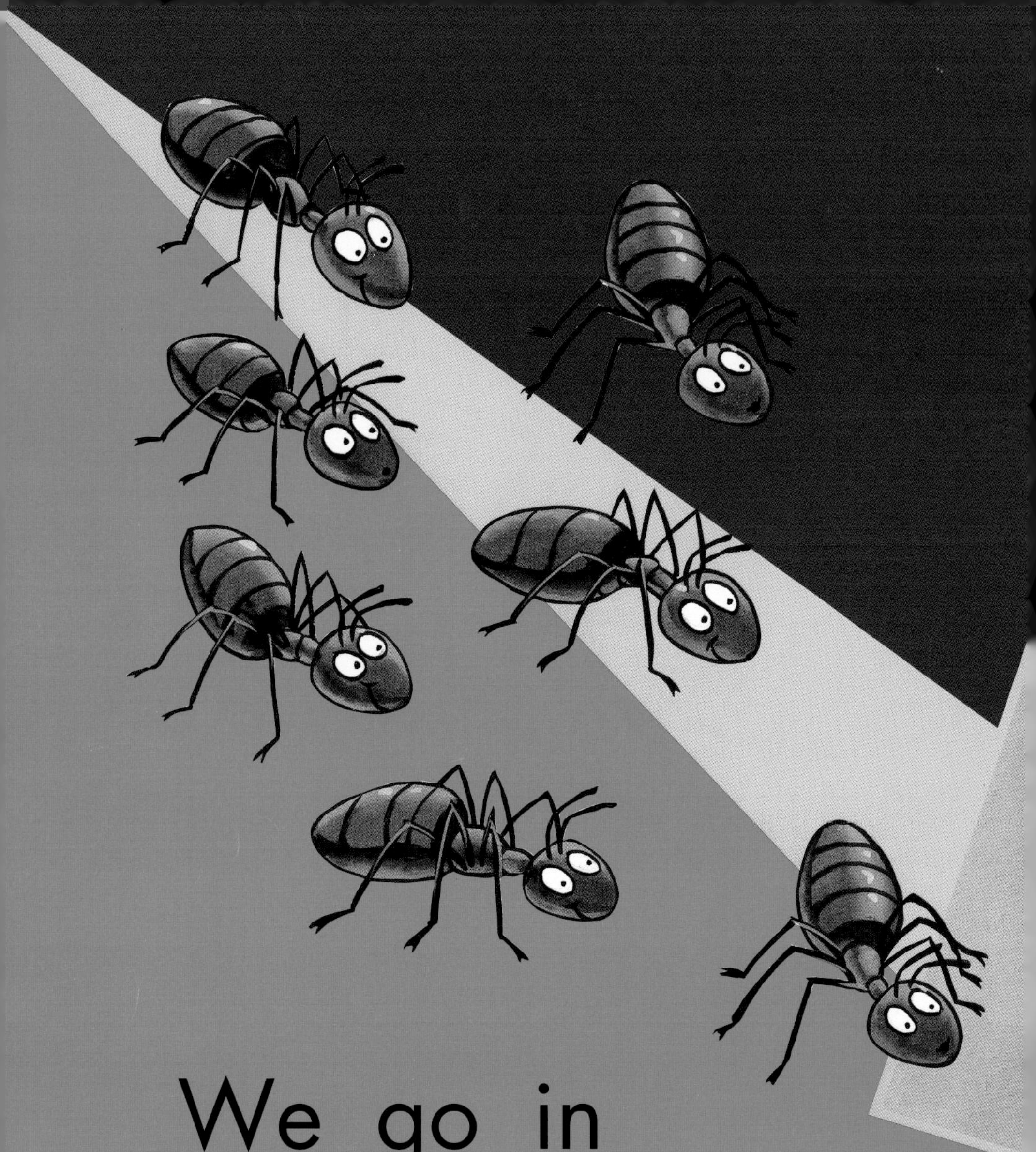

We go in
the watermelon.

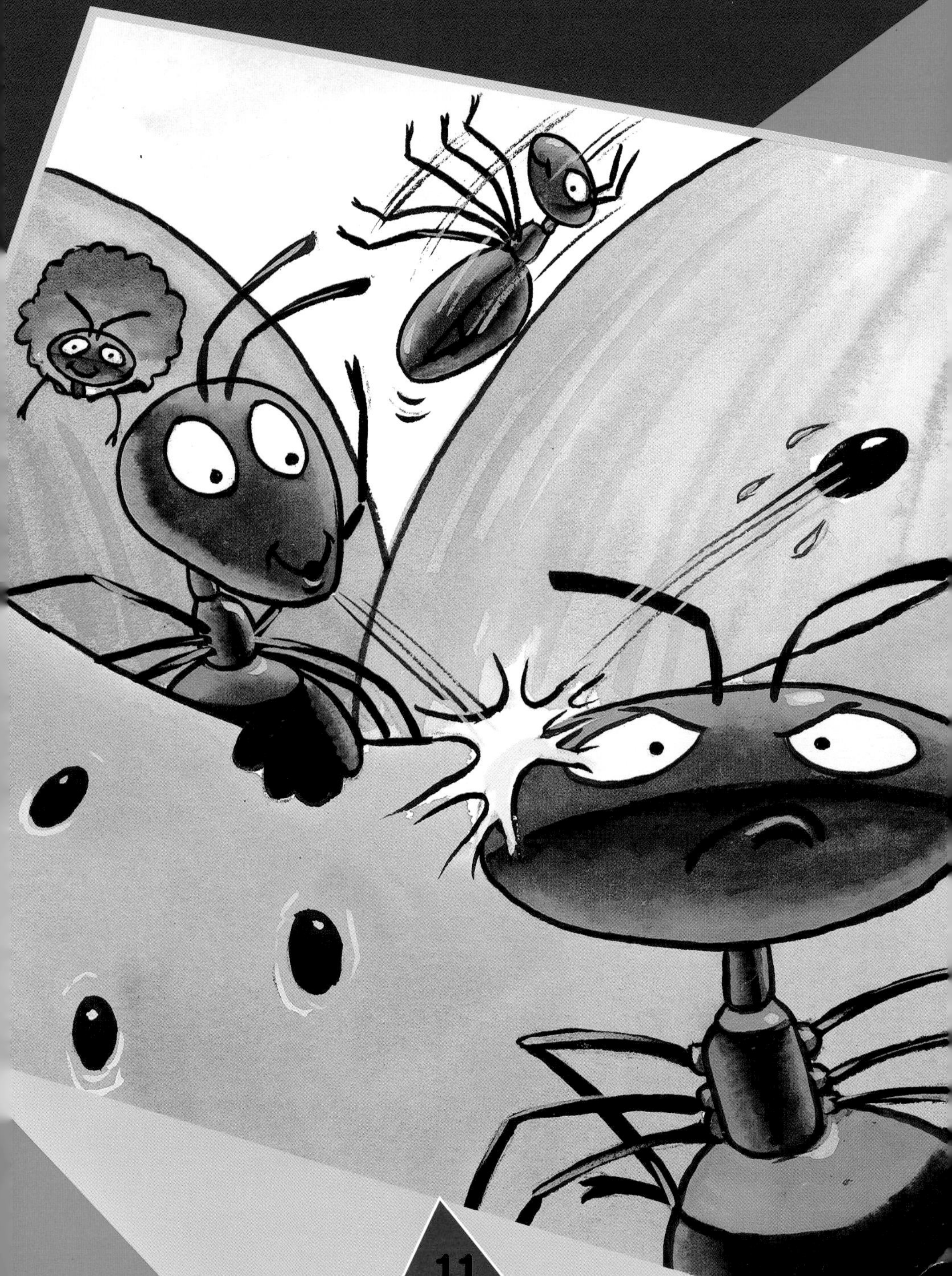

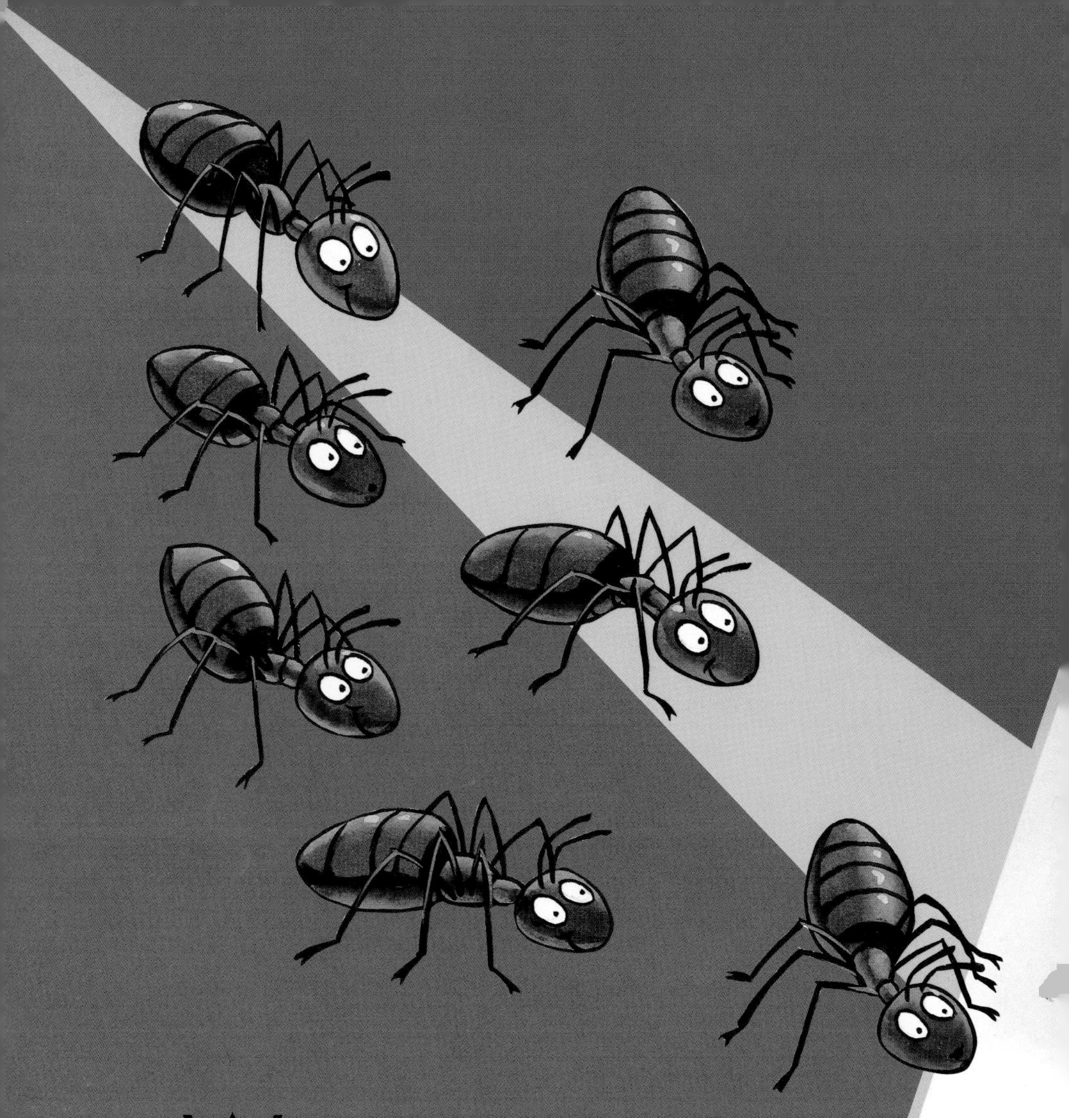

We go in
the ice cream.

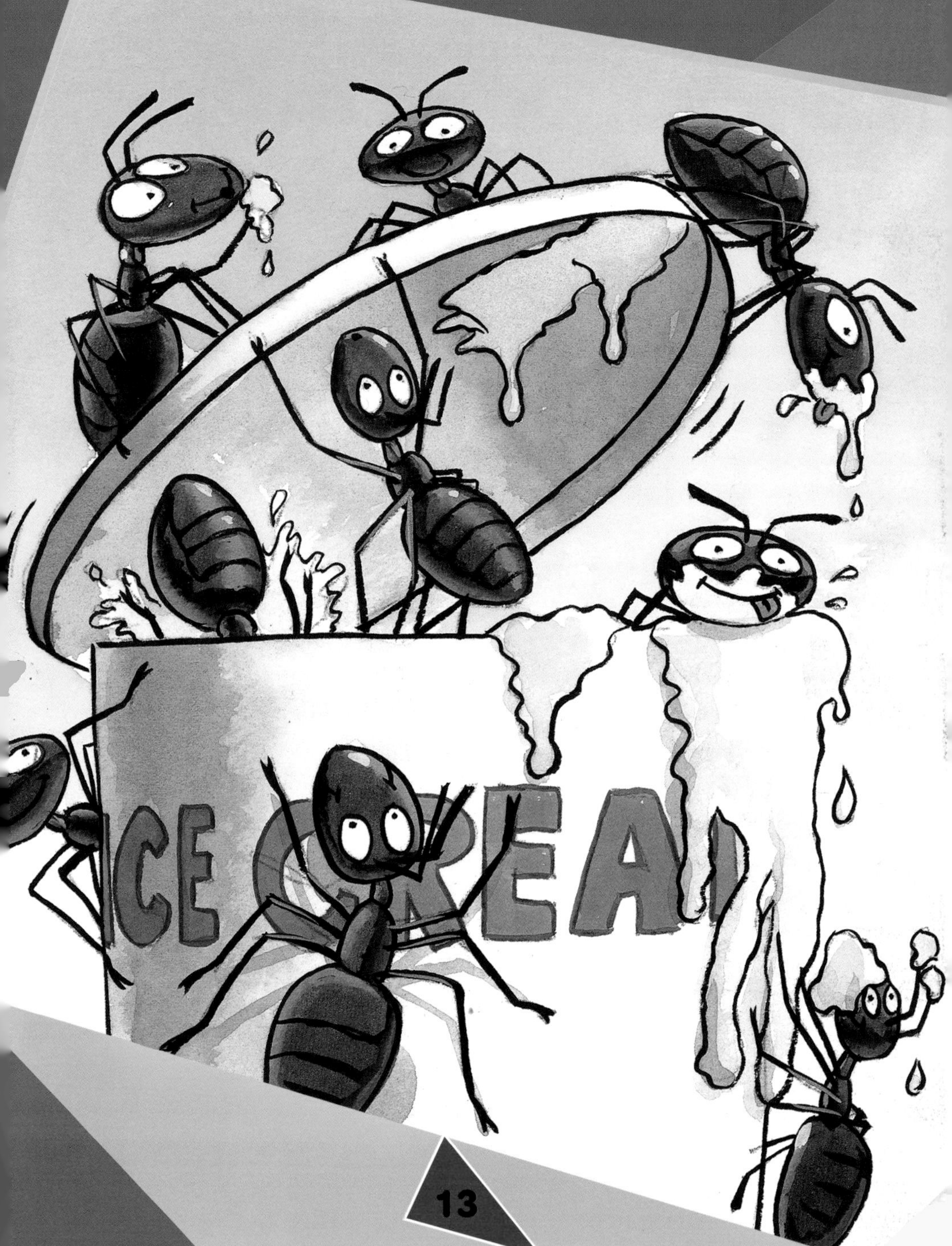
ICE CREA

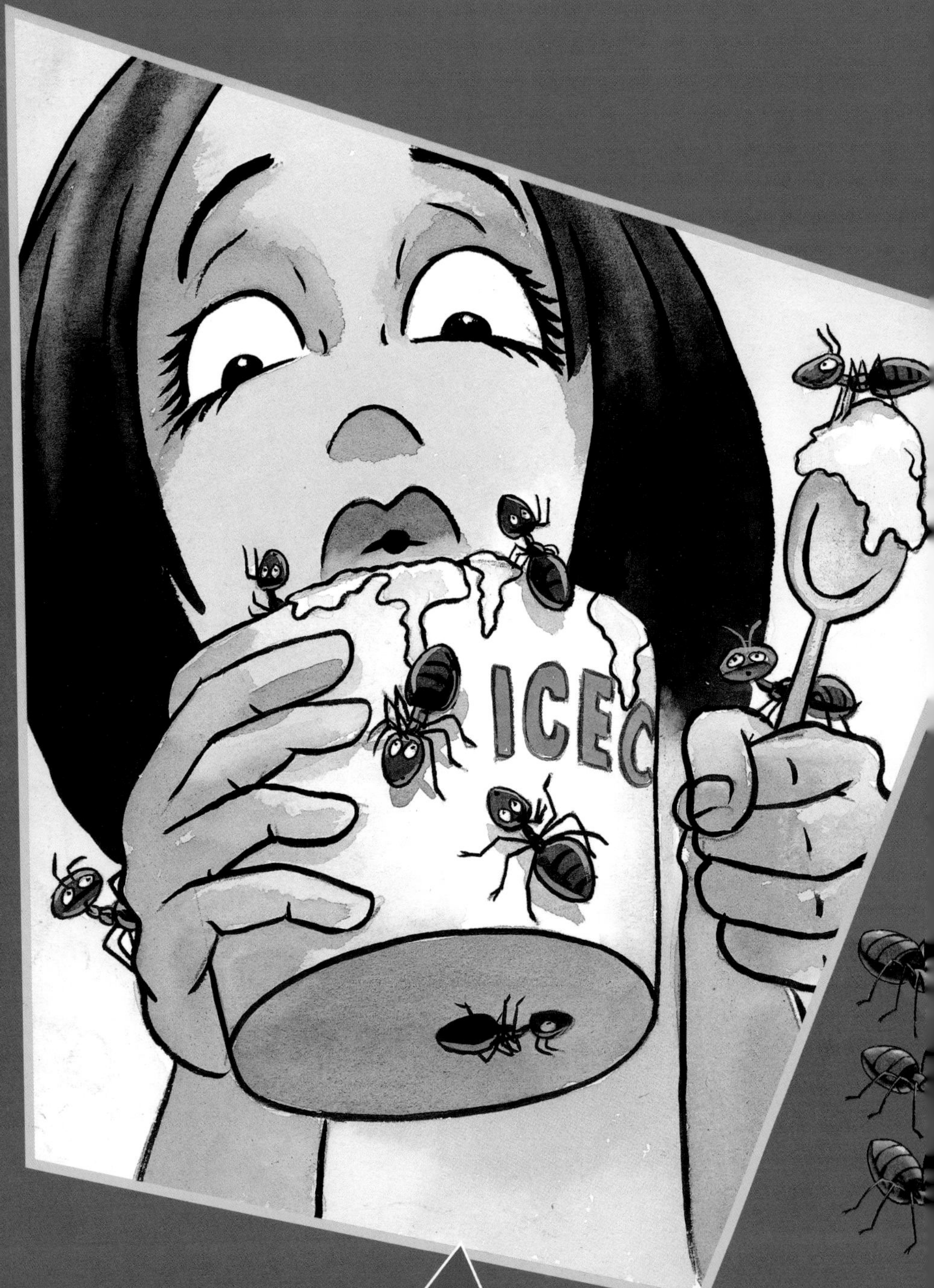
ICEC

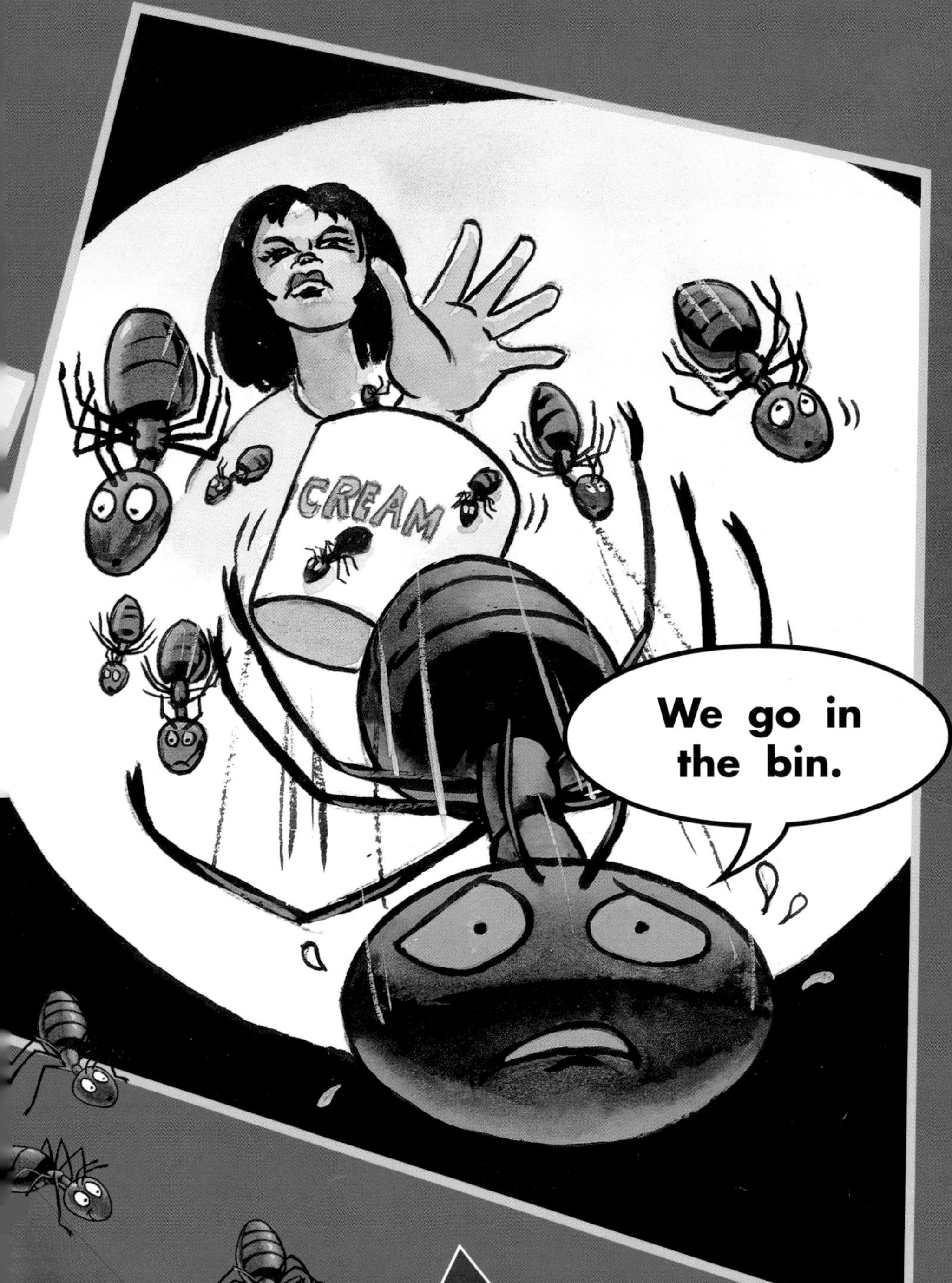
CREAM
We go in the bin.

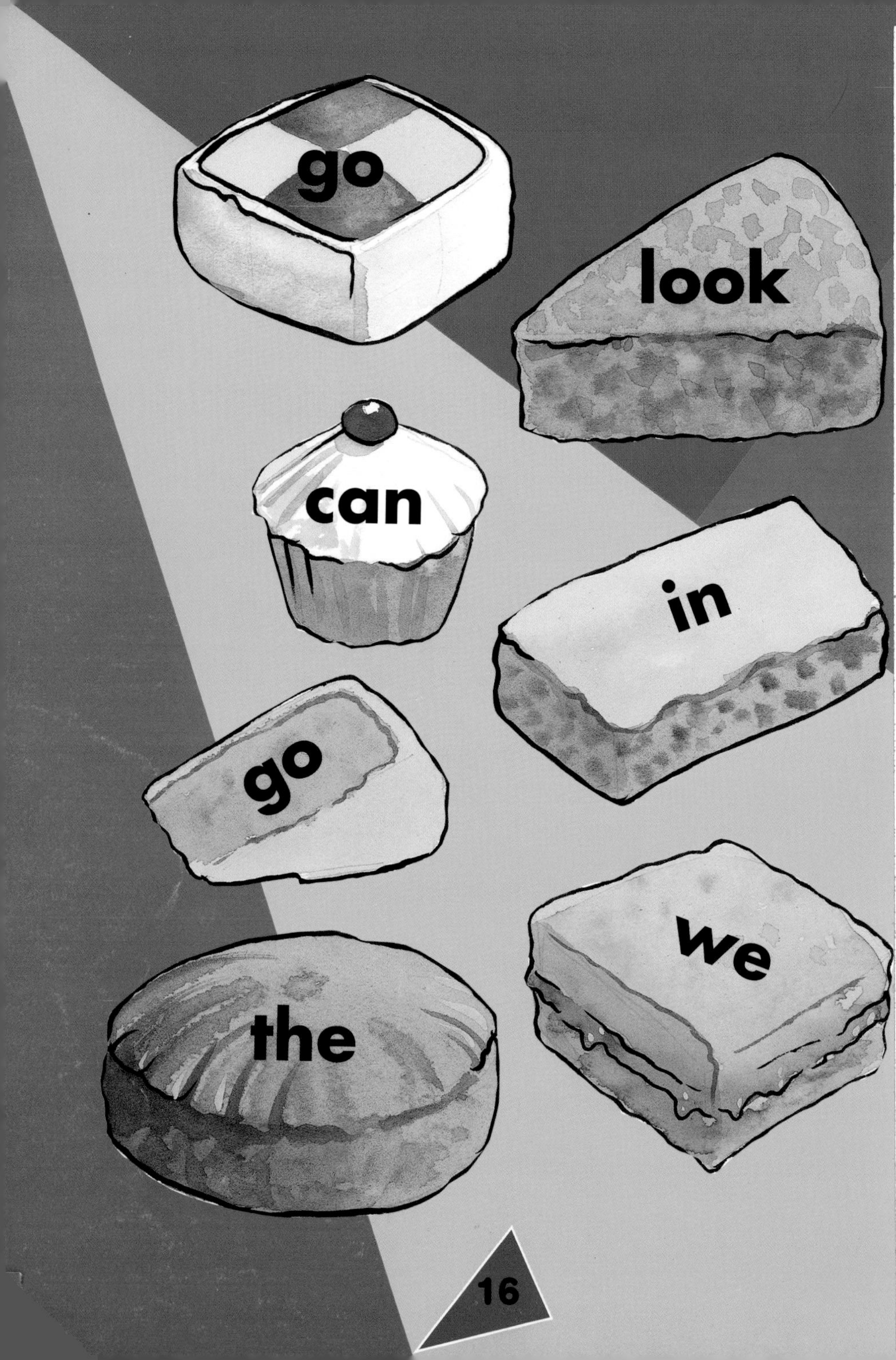
go
look
can
in
go
we
the